Introduction

Since the mid-1980s, the fact that child sexual abuse (CSA) happens and has always happened has been acknowledged increasingly in the public domain as well as in our churches.[1]

Much has rightly been done since then to raise awareness of issues of child protection and to prevent child abuse. The Children Act of 1989 is one key piece of legislation designed to protect children in our society. Within the church, the Church of England and other mainstream denominations all have child protection policies, as do individual churches. Many require declarations from any who work with children that they have no history of child abuse. Training is given to many professionals, including clergy, about preventing and recognizing abuse.

All this is excellent. But despite it all, no-one imagines that child sexual abuse has ceased—either within or outside the church. Cases continue to come to light. Many of these took place several years or even decades ago. Those who were sexually abused as children are today grown-up. Not surprisingly, some of these adult survivors are in our churches. And the word 'survivors' is significant. It indicates that a person has come

'Survivor' is seen as a positive term, indicating that a person has come through an ordeal

through an ordeal. It is therefore seen as a positive term. Some, however, prefer the term 'victim' to indicate that the abuse was not their fault. Others reject this, not denying that they were victims, but wanting to move beyond a designation which they see as being too passive a term which can perpetuate a victim mentality. As we turn to look now at statistics, it is important to remember that, whether victims or survivors, they are, above all, people.

Statistics for Child Sexual Abuse

Statistics are notoriously difficult to interpret, but recent figures suggest 1 in 4 girls and 1 in 9 boys are abused in childhood.[2] There is no reason to believe that this figure is not reflected in our churches, because, contrary to common assumption, sexual abuse is not confined to specific groups in society. Geographical, educational, social, racial and even religious factors are largely immaterial. In fact, and again perhaps contrary to expectations, there is even some evidence that in conservative Christian homes where there is an ethos of discipline, obedience to authority and rigid codes of moral behaviour, the likelihood of abuse is actually greater.[3] What appears significant here is that abuse often happens to children from emotionally distant homes, children who are more in need of affection and thus more vulnerable to the 'grooming' advances of a sexual molester.[4]

There is some evidence that in conservative Christian homes the likelihood of abuse is actually greater

So statistically, in a congregation of one hundred, about eighteen will have had some experience of sexual abuse as children. Of these, some will have come to terms with it, others may still be struggling with its effects. Some may never have told anyone, and some may have so repressed the memories that it has yet to surface in their consciousness. All have survived.

Definition of Sexual Abuse

What do we mean by 'child sexual abuse'? How do we know whether what someone describes 'counts' as abuse? The following definition highlights some key features relevant in relation to adult survivors:

Child sexual abuse is any type of sexual exploitation of a child or adolescent by any older person or adult for the stimulation and/or gratification of that person, which is not necessarily confined to physical contact and which may range from exhibitionism or involvement with pornography to full intercourse or child prostitution; where the developmentally immature victim lacks the authority or power to prevent her/himself being coerced into activities to which she/he is unable to give informed consent, which she/he does not properly comprehend, but which—either at the time or later—the victim considers sexually abusive.[5]

Significant features include:

- It may be an older sibling or adolescent who abused, not an adult. Some survivors try to dismiss abuse perpetrated by someone other than an adult as 'their fault.'

- Sexual abuse ranges in terms of degree of interference. A 'one-off' incident may be as traumatic for the victim as repeated abuse. No

Surviving Child Sexual Abuse

Supporting Adults in the Church

Jeanette Gosney

Tutor in Practical Theology, Trinity College, Bristol

GROVE BOOKS LIMITED
RIDLEY HALL RD CAMBRIDGE CB3 9HU

Contents

Preface

This booklet draws on research carried out for an MPhil, which focused on female Christian survivors of child sexual abuse. There may therefore be a bias towards females, but I nevertheless believe that the insights and observations I set out here can also be applied to male survivors.

Acknowledgments

With thanks to all those who over the years have encouraged me in my thinking, writing and praying about child sexual abuse, and with particular thanks to all those survivors who have allowed me to share in their journeying towards redemption.

The Cover Illustration is by Peter Ashton

First Impression September 2002
ISSN 0144-171X
ISBN 1 85174 508 4

abuse is 'minor,' though adults may feel ashamed that they still struggle with the effects of 'just a flash in the park.'

- Consent must be informed. A child may have said 'yes' to it, but the power differential and their immaturity means that consent can never be 'informed.' The issue of consent is actually irrelevant. The situation should never have arisen in the first place.

- Abuse is defined by the abused person's perception, either at the time or later, not by an outsider's judgment. This point is important for those whose memories of the abuse surface only later, often well into adulthood.

The above has begun to open up the world of survivors, many of whom feel silenced or unheard or at best think they are perceived by society—and the church—as a pastoral problem or 'case' for prayer. Chapters two and three of this booklet invite the church to listen to what Christian survivors have said about the effects of abuse on them so that, albeit from a distanced perspective, we may begin to empathize with their experience, however hard it is to hear. Chapter four then reflects theologically on the issues raised, exploring images of hope towards redemption. In the light of this, chapter five offers a challenge to the churches to look at our practice so that we increasingly embody in our pastoral care and worship more of what it means to be the redeemed and redeeming community of God.

2

Listening to the Voices— The Effects of Abuse

Most of the time most survivors are indistinguishable in the community as survivors. They work, have friends and families and contribute to church life in many different ways. Yet many carry the effects of their abuse into their adult lives—consciously or subconsciously.

For some, especially those who begin to face the past only in adulthood, there are times (which may last several years) when the effects threaten to overwhelm. It is during these times that survivors particularly need the understanding of their church. They may be having professional counselling, but the role of the church in supporting them through therapy is crucial. But even survivors who have come to terms with their past still need understanding from those around them. From time to time they too may struggle with some of the issues below, particularly where these are deeply ingrained patterns of thinking and behaviour.

Recognizing some of the results of CSA is the first stage in being able to offer appropriate support

Recognizing some of the results of CSA is the first stage in being able to offer appropriate support. Some of the effects will be recognized as also being effects of other types of abuse or distressing circumstances such as bereavement or serious illness. Some are apparently contradictory—one survivor may react in the polar opposite way to another, though for the same reason. It is often the intensity or extremeness of a reaction which is significant, rather than the reaction itself. Not all the effects will apply to every instance of abuse, but most of the effects will probably be recognized in some of their forms by most survivors. Equally, the presence of some of the effects does not mean that a person has been abused. They are simply indicators which may suggest abuse if several are identified in one person.

This chapter outlines some common effects under two main headings—the survivor's self-understanding and their relationships with others. It invites us to listen to the survivor's experience.

1. Effects on the Survivor's Self-Understanding

Physical: Attitudes to the body
Survivors often despise their body, which they see as that which betrayed them. It did after all respond and in some way enjoy the touch and stimulation. They may hate looking at themselves in the mirror and see themselves as 'a shapeless blob.' Care of the body—such as hair care, make-up—may be poor, reflecting both their rejection of the body and a desire not to be attractive and encourage unwanted sexual attention. Similarly, they may dress in baggy clothes so that their shape is hidden. They may feel their body is permanently 'polluted' and damaged, so that washing becomes a pointless task because nothing can remove the stain. Conversely, some may shower in extra hot water or be fastidious in other ways about cleanliness, trying to wash away the pollution. They may always dress immaculately—a mask and protective covering for the way they really feel about themselves.

Some turn to self-harm to 'punish' their body (and themselves) for its 'sin,' or become anorexic or bulimic to try to exert some control over it. Comfort eating often fills them with disgust but expresses their craving for love. Many struggle with the fact that they have natural sexual, sensual feelings and desires for touch. But any touch, however 'innocent,' may trigger flashbacks or simply an indefinable dis-ease, leaving the survivor embarrassed or confused. Some find that any thought of sexual intimacy is abhorrent, others want it but are overwhelmed with panic when it happens, others again indulge almost promiscuously in it with a sense that all they are good for is being an object of another's sexual desire.

Emotional/psychological effects
Survivors feel fundamentally negative about themselves and lack basic self-confidence. They carry within their deep consciousness a guilt and shame for being who they are—'bad.' The result is that they often readily blame themselves for everything that happens. They are always apologizing, as if apologizing for existing. They are self-critical—too this, too that, 'stupid,' 'weak,' 'pathetic.' Listening to a person's self-talk often reveals verbal self-abuse.

They may be extremely competent perfectionists, driving themselves to iron out the slightest cause for criticism, trying desperately to cover the 'truth' of their rottenness within. They are deeply anxious about others' perceptions of them. Any criticism of what they *do* is heard as criticism of who they *are*, and is received as rejection, even if rationally they know that the criticism is justified. They may fear to offer their own opinions until they have worked out what is expected of them. Because of their belief that they are unworthy, they cannot believe that anyone will want to spend time with or money on them. So asking for and receiving help can also be extremely difficult. Receiving positive affirmation is as hard as receiving criticism, because it challenges their perception of being 'no good.' Yet they also have a desperate need for approval. If they have risked doing something in public (for example leading intercessions), silence from others is heard as a negative response rather than as simple acceptance. They fear they 'got it wrong.'

The result of all this is often intense loneliness, which confirms their belief that they are 'unloved and unlovable.' They feel 'different.' It is as if a pane of glass separates them from the rest of the world. Somehow the abuse has set them apart, isolating them into a world of their own which simply does not connect with others. So socializing may be hard. They often oscillate between being withdrawn and 'anti-social' (for which they berate themselves as failures) and being apparently bright and cheerful, although this can be an exhausting pretence at being 'normal.' Within their own interior world there is a constant search for their lost self. 'Who am I?' they ask, with a sense of knowing that somewhere deep down is the lost innocent child buried alive. Sometimes they may act childishly, arousing surprise and embarrassment from the adult world they now inhabit. They may also retreat into a fantasy world where it feels safe and offers a brief respite from the exhaustion of trying to fit into a world where they feel they do not belong.

> They feel 'different'; it is as if a pane of glass separates them from the rest of the world

2. Effects on Relationships with Others

Family relationships
Relationships within the family will differ significantly depending on where the abuse took place, who was the abuser and how (if at all) the abuse was dealt with at the time. For example, abuse by the father[6] may leave survivors feeling hatred towards the abuser and resentment and disappointment towards the mother or other siblings for their failure to act (whether or not they knew the abuse was happening). Abuse by an 'outsider' (such as a babysitter, choir leader, teacher, member of the clergy or other authority figure) which was acknowledged may still leave survivors bitter that the parents failed to protect them or, on the other hand, may draw a family together. There may be a general lack of trust between family members. Years of keeping secrets, sometimes of knowing but remaining silent, means that family relationships in adulthood may remain distant and superficial. There may, however, be a sense of solidarity between siblings as silenced co-sufferers in the face of abuse.

If survivors marry, relationships within their family may also vary. Sexual intimacy with the spouse may trigger flashbacks and fear, however much adult survivors rationally trust and love their partners. This may cause frustration, hurt and confusion for both partners which may need to be worked through with professional help. Sometimes survivors do not tell the spouse about the abuse until after marriage, and even then may remain silent, partly through fear of rejection as 'soiled goods,' partly wanting to 'put it in the past' and 'start afresh.' Distressing responses to touch and intimacy may then cause even more difficulties in the relationship. There may be an over-protective attitude towards their children. Survivors often harbour an underlying fear that they are inadequate parents, particularly when the baby will not stop crying, teenagers rebel or something else 'goes wrong.' Their lack of self-worth is inevitably reflected in other relationships.

The wider community
Perhaps not surprisingly, the world at large can seem a daunting place. Survivors are often very sensitive to harshness and apparently uncaring attitudes of others, particularly of those in authority. They often want to rescue all who are hurting and to 'put things right' so that the world becomes a safe place. There may be a deep anger within which stirs when others are perceived as abusing their power and trampling on the vulnerable. Seeing people silenced or humiliated resonates strongly with survivors' own past, and can often result either in a passionate campaign for justice, or in withdrawal because the world feels unsafe and threatening. Fear of new places, of using public transport, of using lifts or being exposed as inadequate in a restaurant all illustrate deep distrust of the environment.

Survivors are suspicious even of people they like—or at least of their own estimation of them

Meeting new people is equally threatening for fear of their rejection or disapproval. Survivors are suspicious even of people they like, or at least of their own estimation of them—can they trust their own evaluations? In the past, it may have been a 'trusted' person who betrayed them by abuse, so as adults they are uncertain about their own ability to judge. Trusting someone sufficiently to disclose anything of their past leaves survivors feeling extremely vulnerable, fearful that their trust will be betrayed in 'gossip,' in 'sharing for prayer,' in disbelief or that people will simply avoid them, leaving them feeling like lepers. They may also be 'labelled' as potential abusers.

Particularly difficult too are relationships with authority-figures, for example at work, and in the church with clergy or group leaders. Those in authority sometimes arouse in the survivors the childhood experience of submission and obedience, a helpless quivering before a power to whom they must bow.

9

Survivors may fear being 'taken for a ride' by people such as financial advisers and salespeople. Daring to express opinions to authority-figures may only be possible at the expense of a huge amount of emotional energy. Survivors are often 'programmed' to expect a violent response to any perceived resistance, in the same way that violence may have met their childhood resistance. So it is easier for survivors to remain in compliant 'child' mode, although this then leaves them feeling frustrated with themselves and patronized. Too often they recognize that yet again they have allowed another to control them. They also often simply want to please. This was sometimes the best way of surviving the abuse. Learnt behaviour in childhood thus becomes a source of disability in relating in the adult world.

But underneath it all, survivors long for affirmation, for someone to respect who, unlike the abuser, will not betray their trust but will restore their confidence in themselves and in humanity.

3 Hearing the Struggle: Survivors, God and the Church

Many Christian survivors (whether or not they come from Christian childhood homes) are challenged to think about their faith and its practice as they face their past and seek to live as committed, faithful Christians.

This is particularly the case if a survivor is working through recently recovered memories of abuse. For many there will be heightened awareness of the church's attitude to issues such as suffering, sin, forgiveness and sexuality. Dealing with some of the issues of sexual abuse explored in the previous chapter is usually distressing in itself, but this distress can be even greater when the survivor's faith, perhaps previously firm, seems to be 'falling apart.'

This chapter explores some of the issues of Christian belief and practice which often arise for survivors. Many of the comments highlight the more negative effects of the church's teaching and the way it is received by survivors. This is *not* to suggest all is negative. Many depend on their church for love and support, and their relationship with God nurtures and sustains them. Rather, it is to raise awareness of some issues of which churches may be unaware. It may make uncomfortable but challenging reading.

Christian Expectations

Survivors want to 'fit in,' and therefore expend huge amounts of energy trying to live up to others' expectations. The following are just some of these expectations relating to church.

Survivors often find themselves under pressure to forgive their abuser immediately. The pressure may come directly from someone in the congregation, or reflect their own understanding about needing to forgive before one can be forgiven, as the Lord's Prayer is often understood. Survivors may speak condemnation to themselves and hear it from others if they are not willing to forgive, and may simply see themselves as hopeless Christians, beyond the forgiveness of God and outcasts in the church community.

Messages in church about sexuality may hinder survivors from coming to terms with their past. There is often an assumption of moral uprightness amongst church members, which implicitly or even explicitly includes sexual purity. Sex may still be linked with sin, which intensifies the survivors' feeling of being guilty and dirty, even if they know rationally that they are the sinned against, not the sinner. Emphases on the virtue of virginity and on needing to confess sexual impropriety to God heighten survivors' sense of shame. Survivors may feel that discussing sexual matters is taboo in Christian circles, so they are reticent about expressing their own fears and struggles on such issues.

Trying to keep up a public front of 'being OK' is exhausting, yet some feel this is the only way to be acceptable

There are myriad expectations surrounding Christian discipleship and witness. Many Christian survivors have absorbed the belief that they should be cheerful and 'rejoice in the Lord always' (Phil 4.4) and therefore feel they are worthless Christians if they are depressed, suicidal or simply overcome with anger and tears. Trying to keep up a public front of 'being OK' is exhausting, yet some feel that is the only way to be acceptable in church. Their sense of shame is greater when they remember biblical teaching about their body being the temple of the Holy Spirit (1 Cor 6.18–20) as they look at the cut marks from their self-harming. Others may feel they are poor disciples because they cannot 'lay everything at the foot of the cross' and 'leave it there' as some would enjoin them to do. Others again are reminded of the verse that they should forget what lies in the past and strive for what lies ahead (Phil 3.13–14)—but cannot simply forget. Thus the overall message they hear and absorb often confirms for them their failure as disciples of Christ.

The overall message they absorb often confirms for them their failure as disciples of Christ

Survivors' struggle with discipleship often includes their personal prayer and Bible study. Many feel they 'ought' to have a regular pattern. Those from an evangelical tradition where the daily 'Quiet Time' is seen as central to Christian practice may struggle to maintain any consistency. For all, former patterns of prayer and Bible study often cease to be helpful, but both survivors and some congregations may see that as failure or 'backsliding.' The Bible can become a source of condemnation rather than healing, or survivors may simply not have the emotional and spiritual energy to read it regularly, which again may induce guilt. This is often the case for those who are feeling particularly hopeless about ever 'recovering' from their past.

Images of God

A common issue for survivors is the tension of believing that God loves them held alongside an image of a God who demands obedience, judges and instils fear of punishment and condemnation. The image of a loving God can feel like a hollow mockery. What sort of loving God allows abuse? The image of a feared, authoritarian figure is often projected onto God from their experience of abuse. Such a God they shy away from. The result can be a sense of guilt, because they know they 'ought' to love and trust God.

Linked with this is sometimes a fear induced by God's 'maleness.' The use of masculine pronouns and strong authority images (King, Ruler) may resonate with the abuse. The omniscience, omnipotence and omnipresence of God, comforting to some, can therefore be a threat—there is 'no escape,' again reflecting the abuse experience (see Ps 139). Doctrines of God's transcendence, splendour and majesty can distance God further. What would such a God want to do with a miserable failure? Thus Ascensiontide can be a difficult festival, with its imagery of glory and power.

However, the closeness or immanence of God can be equally threatening, though longed for. The wonder of a holy, pure God coming close—and becoming polluted by their uncleanness—often appals survivors. They both want and do not want to be 'touched' by God. It is this paradox which distresses them, as well as their capacity, which they often recognize, to turn any 'positive' doctrine into a negative against themselves. Again paradoxically, the God survivors fear may also be the only 'person' with whom they can trust their deepest feelings, knowing (with occasional doubt) that God will not reject them.

In thinking about the Trinity, God as Father clearly causes difficulty for some, particularly those abused by their fathers. For others, however, it is a relief to have a 'Father in heaven' to replace their human father. The Father who apparently sanctioned the abuse of God's own Son can also be an unhelpful image. Singing 'Father, we love you' and of a Father who 'turns his face away' from the suffering, abused Son may simply be too painful.

The person of Jesus is often more helpful, with survivors relating to his suffering as a victim, his bias to the rejected and marginalized, his affirmation of women and his acceptance of children. His humanity—his incarnation—is thus often more important than seeing him as God, although at times it is precisely his humanity which stirs uncomfortable feelings if the relationship becomes sexualized. Jesus' invitation to 'Come to me' (Mt 11.28) and talk of Jesus as Lover whose embrace we long for (Mk 9.36) may not always be welcome. Many contemporary songs express intimacy and the I-Thou relation between the worshipper and Jesus, which can touch deep longings and simultaneously arouse deep fears.

The wonder of a holy, pure God coming close— and becoming polluted by their uncleanness— often appals survivors

Images of the Holy Spirit are less problematic because they are less personal. However, survivors can be frightened by understandings of the Spirit as overwhelming, unpredictable power (Acts 2), because it leaves them feeling helpless and overpowered, again mirroring the abuse experience. The season of Pentecost and some of the more charismatic churches which regularly invite the Holy Spirit in times of public 'ministry' can therefore be difficult for some survivors. The gentleness of the Spirit as Comforter and Counsellor (Jn 14.15) are more positive images for many.

Public Worship

Services can be difficult simply because they are public events, perhaps with people the survivor does not know well. There is often pressure to conform, for example by clapping or raising hands in worship. Services can open survivors to God's healing touch, but this may be simultaneously welcomed and frightening. It can simply make the survivor want to flee in panic. But flight may also meet with disapproval or not be easily possible. So at times survivors may feel they cannot risk church, and stay at home, where they are safe, but often sad.

The words of some hymns and songs can be intensely personal and visual in their imagery. Survivors sometimes find they can no longer sing them. God may not feel like the 'faithful One' who 'lifts them up when they fall down' and survivors may not want to be 'held close' by the 'power of God's love,' though the vision of a God whose 'tenderness' will 'melt all their ugliness' may touch their heart with longing. The children's song 'Lord, you put a tongue in my mouth' can be impossible to sing. Being asked to 'praise God from whom all blessings flow' and to celebrate the victory of Christ over sin when they are angry with God can feel hypocritical. Easter can therefore be a festival which has a hollow ring. Thanking God for his faithfulness and protection over the years (for example 'Lord, for the years,' 'Great is thy faithfulness') may arouse anger or deep despair.

At times survivors may feel they cannot risk church, and stay at home, where they are safe, but often sad

Holy Communion services may leave survivors facing a whole mixture of emotion. The images of sacrifice and victim arouse both empathy and anger. Blood to cleanse may be unhelpful if blood was involved in the abuse, likewise having the bread or wafer placed on the tongue may trigger painful memories if oral sex was part of the experience. The Peace may be another difficult moment where survivors' personal space may be invaded, particularly if hugs are shared. It is again the sense of being out of control that unnerves survivors, making them feel even more a misfit in the community.

Finally, many churches offer a specific ministry of healing or prayer, sometimes as an integral part of every service, sometimes less frequently. This may involve physical touch, which survivors may want to avoid, although this then leaves them sad that they have excluded themselves from something they actually want. Risking allowing others to pray for them is fraught with tension. Survivors speak of times when people have imposed their own prejudices such as praying for 'deliverance from a demon of lesbianism or depression,' or asking that the survivor may be 'covered in the blood of Jesus.' The issue is often one of inappropriate language, but sometimes also expresses a basic ignorance of the situation. There is fear too that people will expect survivors to be 'healed' immediately. So to ask for prayer every time will lead to comments suggesting they ought to be 'claiming their healing,' or 'pulling themselves together.' In healing services as in all services the deep longing is to receive and know God's love. But the very idea of love has been twisted by the abuse. It can be redeemed, but survivors often ask, 'How long, O Lord, how long?'

Reflecting on the Experience: Theological Understandings

4

The church proclaims a gospel of redemption in Christ, a message of God's healing grace.

Using a framework of three movements—from diminution to restoration, isolation to reconciliation and domination to liberation—this chapter explores a range of theological images, Christian perspectives and biblical stories which may provide new ways of understanding this hope of redemption. It offers insights to survivors and to those who support them pastorally as they journey, however haltingly, from despair towards healing.

From Diminution Towards Restoration

Survivors have fundamentally lost their sense of being made in the image of God. They no longer 'walk tall,' but instead walk with eyes to the ground. They want to shrink away, hide, disappear. Diminution.

Shame and Guilt

The place of shame in their lives is crucial. Shame has been described as 'the ongoing premise that one is fundamentally bad, inadequate, defective, unworthy or not valid as a human being,' and an experience which 'involves self-exposure, the sense that one has been stripped bare, rendered naked, exposed to the critical gaze of those who happen to be present' and to oneself.[7] Abuse violates a survivor's essential dignity as one created good in the image of God (Gen 1.26). Abuse belittles—makes small, diminishes a person in their own eyes. They cannot believe they are a child of God. So like Adam and Eve they want to hide.

Yet unlike Adam and Eve, survivors have committed no sin, although when they were children they came to believe that they had. They blamed themselves and felt guilty. In time they come to believe that they have both *done* 'bad things' (guilt, sin) and *are* bad (shame), and this shapes their identity. So they say the confession in church, but it only addresses real guilt, 'guilt that needs confession,' of which they are innocent. Theirs is a false guilt, a 'guilt that needs therapy,' which is in fact their shame.[8] There is usually no liturgical means of dealing with that. So week after week they carry the deep-seated belief that they are guilty sinners.

Violated Boundaries

Abuse violates boundaries—physical and emotional. As children, survivors no longer knew how much of themselves was sacred and belonged to them, how much was accessible, allowing others to penetrate their space. So while outwardly they are 'whole,' inwardly they have no sense of inner confidence and security. Smedes writes: 'If we have no privacy, we have no sacredness; we lose our boundaries, and we have no place within that is holy to ourselves. Take away our sacredness, and we lose our core.'[9] There is a loss of identity. There are parallels with the torture of prisoners: 'the larger the prisoner's pain, the smaller the prisoner's world and therefore, by comparison, the larger the torturer's world.'[10] Survivors have been engulfed in a huge ogre-like world, their sacred space taken away. Their very selves have been forcefully entered, sometimes physically, always emotionally, so there is nothing left of their selves to be treasured and offered to others or to God. They have become no-thing, at best objects of others' desires. And no-one can know their pain. Pain is invisible. Even if they tried to tell, their pain may have been belittled: 'He was only playing with you'; 'It wasn't that bad.' So they shrink into a corner, sometimes literally.

So how might their shattered identity be restored? How might they come to know again their selves as those made in the image of God?

Mirroring Goodness

Aquinas' theory of goodness affirms both that God alone is perfect goodness, but also that all creatures, as beings made in the image of God, participate to some degree in God's goodness (Gen 1.31). Furthermore, every creature is oriented towards its own goodness.[11] Here is something of hope in God—movement towards a fullness, a kernel of goodness which can be fanned into growth. It affirms that survivors do not have to be determined by what others have said or done. The hope for change is within them, God-given.

But if survivors no longer believe this truth, it needs to be mirrored to them. We all need to experience positive mirroring, where the self is affirmed and reflected back by the other as being good, loved and valuable. Capps believes that mirroring is at the heart of the Christian gospel as 'the form and means by which the depleted self experiences divine grace, the blessing of God: May the Lord's face shine upon you' (Num 6.24–26, 2 Cor 3.16–18).[12] This may, of course, be through friends. So when survivors, eyes usually lowered in shame, risk looking into the face of God or of others, they see themselves. Their essential goodness is mirrored back as Goodness shines onto them. Their shame is overcome through others' affirmation. They become the reflection—the image of Goodness, God's beloved, in whom God is well-pleased (Mark 1.11, 9.7).

Remembering the Christ-child

Survivors need to find the damaged child within, the 'child that was once born whole, full of the grace of loving and needing love.'[13] In the image of the divine Child there is room for survivors to see themselves as vulnerable and fragile and yet with strength and capacity to love and trust. As survivors recognize the anger and anguish of their damaged child, so they also begin to empathize with their vulnerability. Reflecting on the Christ-child allows survivors to nurture and restore their inner child towards wholeness. Grey writes of growing into wholeness through re-membering, 'painfully putting together the fragmented bits of self' as they surface.[14] Christ is imaged as the Reminder to survivors that they are made in the image of God. Thus the violation of boundaries, the tearing open and fragmentation which destroyed the sense of self can in and through Christ be restored. The Christ-child meets the child within and calls it forth from its corner to become the child of God it was created to be: holy and loved. Survivors re-member who they are. Their identity is restored.

From Isolation Towards Reconciliation

Survivors are isolated—body and mind alienated from each other, estranged from others by the awkwardness they feel at making relationships, distanced from a transcendent God.

Pollution and Taboo

Survivors feel polluted, whether or not the sexual abuse was physical. Pollution can be seen as dirt. In anthropological terms, '...dirt is essentially disorder. There is no such thing as absolute dirt: it exists in the eye of the beholder.'[15] Survivors 'behold' themselves as dirty. Their 'disordered' state does not belong in ordered society. They may reject their body because they cannot find a way of dealing with the dirt. This is particularly so when the abuse remains secret. Social and religious structures and taboos prevent the dirt—internalized as guilt or sin—from being brought into the open for ritual cleansing. Sacrifice cannot be made (contrast Leviticus 1–7). Survivors must remain alienated from themselves and, from their perspective, also from others and from God. They cannot enter the sanctuary of God, the holy of holies; they cannot approach the throne of grace. The profane must not sully the sacred. Isolation.

Loss of Intimacy

Survivors have often learnt not to feel the pain of betrayal, the longing for love, the enjoyment of touch. Emotions as children became confused and distorted—perhaps enjoying sensually the intimacy, but deeply disturbed and fearful of the context. The result can be 'an emotional snow fort,'[16] which of course removes from consciousness not only the painful emotions, but also those emotions which are life-affirming. The emotional freeze—the fear of any intimacy and allowing themselves to be known—impoverishes their God-given capacity to relate to others. They may struggle to make friends. They may lose connection with God, the Friend and Companion. They simply dare not risk believing that passages in the Bible about God's love and compassion (such as Hosea 11, Isaiah 43 and 54) might include them. Hope hurts. It is safer to be a fugitive—or even to condemn themselves as excluded from God's love because they cannot risk loving (1 John 4.7ff). It is an existence, but not life in all its fullness.

So if this is the state of the survivor—isolation, alienation, estrangement— how can it be transformed? What images speak of reconciliation?

'The holiest of temples'
'The abuse of a person can be seen as the abuse of the holiest of temples.'[17] We might reflect on Jesus entering the temple and overturning the money-changers' tables (John 2.12ff) and see it as demonstrating God's anger at the violation of the sacredness of the human body in sexual abuse.[18] There are times when survivors need to know the strength of God's rage at the abuse and his determination to fight passionately and compassionately for them. He will not remain silent. He will act. The survivor's dirt will be removed. God will cleanse the temple.

'This is my body'
In incarnation Jesus becomes an object of touch who feels, eats, shares bread and in communion allows himself 'to be taken in…as the object of sustenance.'[19] In Jesus, God is revealed not as distant, disembodied, but incarnate, embodied Companion. Human flesh is sacred. And in Communion survivors remember that Jesus is the one who like them has known abuse and humiliation and betrayal. His body was broken—but not rejected—by God. Thus as survivors feed on Christ, they can begin to know the healing of their own wounds, no longer seeing them as rejected by God. In the sharing of Communion, there is reunion; God and humanity at one.

'You are my friends'
The image of Jesus as Friend is generally positive for survivors. Vulnerability is key here. Vulnerability includes an openness to being wounded, which for survivors brings terror. It risks intimate, personal disclosure to one's self and to an other. It asks to be honoured.[20] Vulnerability risks crossing boundaries—social and religious—and in the transcending of those boundaries, barriers of shame, humiliation and fear fall away and love triumphs. Jesus' life and death reveal moments of intense intimacy and vulnerability, an invitation to trust and be trusted. In his encounters with outcasts (Lk 7.36ff; 8.43ff;

18

13.10ff; 17.11) we see both Jesus and those he met taking risks. Jesus risked breaking social taboos and religious codes of conduct. Those who came to him risked further ostracization. It is in these tableaux that we see a model of friendship which has a quality of 'fierce tenderness' which is deep, accepting and committed to the care of the other.[21] Fierce tenderness says: 'I am for you.' Jesus' fierce tenderness was costly—supremely so on the cross—and through it people were touched into new life. In time, as trust in self, others and God grows, it gives survivors a new dignity and sense of worth. There is inner and outward reconciliation. God in Jesus is increasingly revealed as a true Friend who calls his followers 'friends' and invites them to go and do as he has done—to risk the vulnerability of loving (Jn 15.13ff).

From Domination Towards Liberation

Many survivors are imprisoned by fear and anger, controlled by learnt behaviours. Other people's expectations dominate them. They are bound in body, mind and spirit.

Imprisoned by Anger

Rage, frustration, resentment—all are expressions of anger. Anger at a person which is not expressed prevents true separation from that person. Thus for survivors still angry with their abuser, there is no escape from the abuser. The past is ever present. Yet society generally disapproves of the expression of anger as a sign of lack of self-control. So survivors tend to repress it further, perhaps displacing it into excessive commitment to work or a hobby. Although God's anger at injustice is clear (Exod 22.22ff, Amos 5.21ff), the message in church is often that anger is a sin (Col 3.8; 2 Cor 12.20). There is a fear of losing God's love if anger is expressed. In church relationships the power of anger is often covered over with 'chronic niceness.'[22] Honest and open relationships are subverted by the denial of anger. So the survivor, trying to be a 'good Christian,' remains locked by Christian culture in a 'prison of hostility,'[23] out of right relation with others and with God.

Bound to Suffering

The notion of suffering as redemptive often removes from survivors any encouragement to break free from a victim mentality. Interpretations of suffering include its value as character-building and as a test of faith. So to resist it seems to be 'failing' as a Christian (Rom 5.3, Heb 12.5ff, 1 Pet 1.6ff). The notion of suffering as punishment for sin (Gen 3.14ff) reinforces survivors' beliefs that they were to blame for the abuse, thus making it more difficult for them ever to place responsibility for it on the abuser. Suffering is also linked with notions of sacrifice and obedience, such as that modelled by Jesus' death in obedience to his Father's will (Heb 5.8). Survivors, having learnt to obey their abuser, now find a way of seeing the obedience and suffering as good. Self-sacrifice is the imitation of Christ, with the promise of future resurrection as reward for present suffering. They become practitioners of 'doormat theology' which allows others to walk all over them. They sacrifice themselves to others' desires, always ready to be helpful. And sadly, sometimes others exploit that. And survivors collude, for it confirms them as they know themselves: people deserving of punishment, called to rejoice in suffering as disciples of Christ (Rom 8.17f, 2 Cor 1.3ff, 2 Tim 1.8, 1 Pet 4.12ff).

Forced to Forgive
The issue of forgiveness, particularly within the Christian community, looms large for many survivors. The problem is not in the generally accepted assertion that forgiving the offender is a positive act which can release the survivor from being 'entwined' with the offender. Rather, the problem resides in a number of misunderstandings about forgiveness. The belief that failure to forgive leaves the survivor 'trapped' in anger can precipitate premature forgiveness by survivors who desperately want to 'be better,' leaving no opening for exploring buried anger or grief. There may be pressure to forgive both because the Bible commands it and because failure to do so leaves the survivor outside God's forgiveness (Mt 6.14f, Lk 6.37, Col 3.13). So survivors may want to forgive at once—and may say they have forgiven—so as to remain acceptable within the faith community and before God. They may also forgive immediately to avoid facing their inner pain, insisting that the issue is closed. For some forgiveness is linked with forgetting—and forgetting is something they can never do. Another issue is the community's attitude to the abuser. When someone's house is burgled, few would immediately expect the victim to forgive. There would be talk of making the guilty party pay. But strangely, even though the horror and disgust at the 'event' may be greater, survivors are often urged to understand abusers as 'troubled individuals,' again suggesting a duty to forgive. The survivors' pain is ignored. They are in fact additionally burdened, crushed by others' expectations.

> *When someone's house is burgled, few would immediately expect the victim to forgive*

If these are some of the interpretations of Christian theology that dominate and imprison a survivor, what understandings might bring release towards liberation?

Releasing Passion
The expression of anger is vital in the process of mourning losses and healing. It is 'the backbone to healing,' 'a powerful transforming energy.'[24] Anger

can be part of love or passion, something which is prepared to act coura-geously to establish communion with another—or with God. Survivors take time to find this energy. Grieving often needs to be done first. But passionate anger can be the energy towards breaking free from victim to survivor. It can become sacred anger, such as that of the prophets who spoke out for justice in the face of oppression, for hope to replace despair. Jesus' anger—or pas-sion—was focused, targeting violated relationships. His whole life was infused with passion for humanity, a passion for transformation to set the captives free (Lk 4.18ff). God can thus become the source and inspiration of this passion, so that the survivor works with God, channelling anger con-structively against social injustices, working for peace and reconciliation. It is such passion that transforms survivors' own suffering. It does not justify their suffering and neither does it remove the scars of suffering. Jesus' wounds were there after his resurrection (Jn 20. 26ff). But from it comes an energy which can be used creatively to shape the future of the wider community. The focus of suffering moves from self to others with a passion that one day there will be an end to all suffering—a vision of the new creation (Rev 21.4).

Freed to Forgive
Forgiveness 'is not merely an act of the will, although it is an intentional, wilful act.'[25] If it were merely an act of the will, it could be demanded and given relatively easily. Forgiveness is a 'letting go process,' a staged rite—which may indeed be marked by different rituals. The process may move from 'Forgiveness? No way!' to 'wanting to want to forgive' to 'wanting to forgive' before forgiveness is finally offered. A first stage may be simply ac-knowledging the hurt and allowing the self to experience the suppressed feelings. Survivors begin to taste the joy of being released from trapped emotions, and want to be free of hatred towards the abuser. So they begin to look at the pain caused by the abuse and to place the responsibility for it with the offender. Forgiveness becomes no longer dismissing the abuse itself, but rather survivors taking authority to free themselves from the abuser's hold. Releasing the abuser to God's justice and mercy, recognizing one's own broken relationships and need of forgiveness, and praying a version of Jesus' prayer 'Father, forgive them, for they know not what they do' (Lk 23.34) may be other stages in the process

Such a letting go takes courage, for it may be changing thought patterns of a lifetime

before at some point perhaps being able to say 'I forgive him/her,' or more rarely the direct 'I forgive you.' Such a letting go takes courage, for it may be changing thought patterns of a life-time. But it brings a freedom that Christ came to give and continues to give through his Spirit (Lk 4.18, 2 Cor 3.17, Gal 5.1).

5

Transforming Practice: Supporting Survivors

Some of the issues raised so far have already pointed to appropriate changes in pastoral support and worship.

This chapter offers some more explicit suggestions for individuals and churches to consider. There are, of course, no 'right' answers, but if at the very least understanding is greater, attitudes are also likely to change, and changed attitudes lead to increased sensitivity. Few survivors want to be treated as 'objects' of another's pastoral care. But by asking about our pastoral practice and worship in relation to survivors, we may discover that we are not only shaping a community more inclusive of them, but one which increasingly becomes in thought, word and deed the community of the Beloved for all.

The Experience of Church

1. Preaching and Teaching on Sexuality and Violence
How often do sermons engage with issues of sexuality, gender, violence and abuse of power? Do home groups or study courses discuss such personal issues at a real level? Occasionally raising the issues breaks down barriers, and makes it feel safer to talk about such topics within the Christian context.

2. Guilt, Shame and Confession
Can thought be given to the time of confession so that both guilt *and* shame can be brought to God? How is the confession introduced? How is 'sin' spoken of? Can it include that which has hurt us as well as ways we have hurt others? And if guilt needs to hear forgiveness and shame needs to hear acceptance, how do we express both in our liturgy? Overall, do we have a balance between emphasizing our sinfulness and our essential goodness? Underlying all this is an invitation to consider how we speak of what Christ has done for us. There are more ways of speaking of atonement than penal substitution, but how often are other images (such as restoration, reconciliation, liberation) explored within congregations?

Do we have a balance between emphasizing our sinfulness and our essential goodness?

3. Touch and Anointing
Stopping all touch is almost certainly too extreme. But how aware are people of its difficulty for some? If touch is offered at a healing service, exactly what is going to happen needs to be explained beforehand—and kept to by those administering it. Anointing on hands or the forehead, for example, can be helpful, but the weight of heavy hands on the head might feel oppressive.

4. Tears and Vulnerability
One survivor talked about feeling comfortable in her new church because 'messiness' was OK. The church she had left was too 'prim and proper.' Engaging with raw reality in prayers and sermons and church involvement with local welfare organizations helps congregations to bring life's 'messiness' into worship and Christian living, and to acknowledge the pain, even with tears and anger. How do we help women and men cope with their emotions? Encouraging the congregation to be honest and vulnerable with each other may need modelling by the leadership. Does it happen—and are there appropriate limits to expressing vulnerability?

Encouraging the congregation to be honest and vulnerable may need modelling by the leadership

5. Songs, Hymns and Language for God
It really is worth looking at the words of the music we use. What images of God are present? A study of some of the vocabulary of our hymns and songs could be a useful exercise for the whole congregation as a way of looking at how we understand God—and might help people to become aware of any imbalances in our language. Similarly in our prayers, how is God addressed—always as 'Father' or 'Almighty,' or sometimes perhaps as 'tender God,' 'creating God'? Encouraging people to think about new ways of addressing God could be part of training for those who lead intercessions.

6. Special Services for Survivors
There are a variety of resources available which can be used and adapted for different settings. Services may be simple short rites for the survivor and a few friends, or may be larger events involving the congregation to pray more generally for issues around sexual abuse. Both may include a time of healing. It is important that any service, however brief, is planned with the survivor(s) as far as possible, rather than the church or vicar controlling. Sensitivity to their needs is paramount. How about planning a service for all those affected by sexual abuse?

Pastoral Support Amongst the Congregation

General Support and Encouragement

Survivors do not usually live as those defined by their abuse, although some-times other people want to keep them in that position. What survivors need is sensitivity to some of the issues they face in everyday life. They may, for example, need encouragement to socialize—a phone call offering a lift, an invitation to join a cinema trip. And do we notice if they have taken a bit of effort with their appearance—and affirm it?

Three positive comments to every negative is a good rule to follow

Survivors may find it hard to take criticism. That does not mean that criticism is never given, but that how it is given and its possible effect is thought about. Three positive comments to every negative is a good rule to follow. Learning to laugh at themselves and disconnect *doing* something wrong from *being* 'wrong' will need gentle nurture.

Learning to have fun is also important. Joy has not always been part of their lives, and survivors can find experiencing positive emotions as hard as ex-pressing the negative. How good are we as churches at celebrating and laughing—even in a service?

Some will need help in expressing opinions. They often do not know what they think, because they learnt it was better to do as they were told. They worry about making a decision. How do we help one another talk over deci-sions? Do we give each other enough time? If we are leading a group, how do we receive sugges-tions from others? Do people feel ignored or put down, or is the idea (however outrageous!) re-ceived graciously?

Survivors may need times to be withdrawn while at other times someone coming alongside is helpful

Survivors may need times to be withdrawn, while at other times someone coming alongside is help-ful. There are no easy answers here. People simply need to try to pick up signals from body language. Survivors sometimes think that people are avoiding them (a bit like people may avoid someone who's been bereaved), yet often they want a 'normal' conversation rather than always talking about 'how they are feel-ing.' How good are we at approaching others? Helping congregations explore their fears in this area could lead to a greater sense of belonging together.

Support and Counsel

Those offering support to survivors who are dealing with the past need to be aware of the amount of time and energy which can be involved and therefore need to be able to set their own boundaries, both for their sake and the survivor's. A supporter who suddenly withdraws leaves the survivor again feeling betrayed. Most people are not trained counsellors. The danger is that people often try to counsel when referral to a professional counsellor would be wiser, while still continuing to support the survivor informally. (Rushing survivors into professional counselling before they are ready can, however, be damaging. The choice must remain with the survivor.) If someone does offer informal support, they need to be aware that dependency can develop. The supporter becomes the longed-for trusted person, and can be seen as either the substitute parent, or the sexual partner who will not abuse. This may happen completely subconsciously, but if allowed to develop causes greater shame when it is finally confronted. Supporters also need to decide how they will deal with some of the distressing material they might hear. There may be legal implications, particularly if the abuser may still be abusing. What are the bounds of confidentiality? Counsellors have supervisers. What about clergy or lay pastoral carers?

Forgiveness and Reconciliation

The issue of forgiveness may be far wider than forgiving the abuser. Discussing the process towards forgiving anyone is crucial, and particularly so if there is any thought of the survivor speaking directly to the abuser. Face-to-face contact may not be wise (or not even possible) so other ways such as writing letters (real or written but never sent) may be preferable. Forgiveness challenges us all. How much do churches teach about forgiving each other and ourselves, rather than always focussing on being forgiven by God? At root, that asks about how we handle disagreements and conflict in church and as Christians. Do we avoid it, or address it honestly?

The Hope of Redemption

We have heard the survivors' experience—and perhaps been able to empathize with it. We have reflected on it theologically. And we have considered ways of responding practically. The question is: what will we do now? It is likely that every one of us knows a survivor of child sexual abuse—whether we realise it or not.

In Christ survivors can hold on to the promises of God's transforming love

My hope is that from this booklet will have come a greater awareness of the issues of sexual abuse which actually affect us all, and that from that awareness will come a growing care for one another—particularly survivors. If we are a church which proclaims redemption and believes that in Christ there is restoration, reconciliation and liberation, we need to take seriously how we live out that faith, so that even those who doubt come to believe (Jn 20.24-29). Will we, as individuals and as churches, commit ourselves to supporting survivors of sexual abuse? To listening to their stories, hearing their pain and in humility and love looking at our own attitudes and practices within the church? Will we commit ourselves to become, with the help of God, an expression and vehicle of Christ's redeeming grace?

There is hope for survivors. Their pain and suffering can be redeemed. In Christ they—like each one of us—can hold on to the promises of God's transforming love. But it would help them if the church could share with them in their journey towards redemption. And that journey can start today—for survivors and for the church. As the song says:

> Behold, behold, I make all things new,
> beginning with you,
> and starting from today.
> Behold, behold, I make all things new,
> my promise is true,
> for I am Christ the way.[26]

Resources

6

Hilary Cashman, *Christianity and Child Sexual Abuse* (London: SPCK, 1993)

Joanne Feldmeth and Midge Finley, *We Weep for Ourselves and our Children: A Christian Guide for Survivors of Childhood Sexual Abuse* (San Francisco: Harper Collins, 1990)

Muriel Green and Anne Townsend, *Hidden Treasure: A Journey towards Healing from Sexual Abuse* (London: DLT, 1994)

Margaret Kennedy, *The Courage to Tell: Christian Survivors of Sexual Abuse Tell their Stories of Pain and Hope* (London: CTBI, 1999)

Alistair McFadyen, *Bound to Sin: Abuse, Holocaust and the Christian Doctrine of Sin* (Cambridge: CUP, 2000)

Patrick Parkinson, *Child Sexual Abuse and the Churches* (London: Hodder and Stoughton, 1997)

James Newton Poling, *The Abuse of Power: A Theological Problem* (Nashville: Abingdon Press, 1991)

Liturgical Resources

Ruth Burgess and Kathy Galloway (eds), *Praying for the Dawn: A Resource Book for the Ministry of Healing* (Glasgow: Wild Goose Publications, 2000)

Kathy Galloway (ed), *The Pattern of our Days: Liturgies and Resources for Worship* (Glasgow: Wild Goose Publications, 1996)

Janet Morley, *All Desires Known* (London: SPCK, 1992)

Hannah Ward and Jennifer Wild, *Human Rites: Worship Resources for an Age of Change* (London: Mowbray, 1995)

Hannah Ward, Jennifer Wild and Janet Morley (eds), *Celebrating Women* (London: SPCK, 1995)

Support Organizations

Christian Survivors of Sexual Abuse, BM-CSSA, London, WC1N 3XX

Churches' Child Protection Advisory Service (CCPAS), PO Box 133, Swanley, Kent BR8 7UQ

Notes

1   The death of Jasmine Beckford in 1985, and the Cleveland cases in 1987 were incidents which raised the public profile of CSA in the UK.
2   Rape Crisis Federation Wales and England, 2001. See: www.rapecrisis.co.uk/ support1.htm
3   See for example D Elliott, 'The Impact of Christian Faith on the Prevalence and Sequelae of Sexual Abuse' in *Journal of Interpersonal Violence*, March 1994, p 105.
4   See for example D Allender, *The Wounded Heart: Hope for Adult Victims of Child Sexual Abuse*, (Farnham: CWR, 1991) p 74f.
5   J Renvoize, *Innocence Destroyed: A Study of Child Sexual Abuse* (London: Routledge, 1993) p 36.
6   It is still generally recognized that sexual abusers are in the large majority of cases male. It is, however, also important to acknowledge that females also abuse others sexually, particularly for the sake of those who have been abused by a female and who might otherwise be a denied and unheard group within society.
7   L Smedes, *Shame and Grace: Healing the Shame We Don't Deserve* (San Francisco: Harper Collins, 1993) p 3. D Capps, *The Depleted Self: Sin in a Narcissistic Age* (Minneapolis: Fortress Press, 1993) p 75f.
8   M Green and A Townsend, *Hidden Treasure: A Journey towards Healing from Sexual Abuse* (London: DLT, 1994) p 83.
9   Smedes, *op cit*, p 61.
10 E Scarry, *The Body in Pain: The Making and Unmaking of the World* (New York: OUP, 1987), p 29ff.
11 J Porter, *The Recovery of Virtue: The Relevance of Aquinas for Christian Ethics* (Louisville: Westminster/John Knox Press, 1990) p 37ff.
12 D Capps, *The Depleted Self: Sin in a Narcissistic Age* (Minneapolis: Fortress Press, 1993) p 64.
13 R Brock, 'And a Little Child will Lead us: Christology and Child Abuse,' in J Brown and C Bohn (eds), *Christianity, Patriarchy and Abuse: A Feminist Critique* (New York: Pilgrim Press, 1989) p 53.
14 M Grey, *Redeeming the Dream: Feminism, Redemption and the Christian Tradition* (London: SPCK, 1989) p 66.
15 M Douglas, *Purity and Danger: An Analysis of the Concepts of Pollution and Taboo* (London: Routledge and Kegan Paul, 1966) p 2.
16 C Poston and K Lison, *Reclaiming our Loves: Hope for Adult Survivors of Incest* (Boston: Little, Brown and Co, 1989) p 34.
17 M Fortune, *Sexual Violence: The Unmentionable Sin* (New York: Pilgrim Press, 1983) p xiii.
18 C Doehring, 'Developing Models of Feminist Pastoral Counselling' in *The Journal of Pastoral Care*, Spring 1992.
19 Scarry, *op cit*, p 214ff.
20 A Thatcher, *Liberating Sex: A Christian Sexual Theology* (London: SPCK, 1993) p 162ff.
21 M Hunt, *Fierce Tenderness: A Feminist Theology of Friendship* (New York: Crossroad, 1992) p 7ff.
22 A Campbell, *The Gospel of Anger* (London: SPCK, 1986) p 60f.
23 *ibid*, p 50.
24 Green and Townsend, *op cit*, p 67.
25 Fortune, *op cit*, p 208.
26 In *Come all you People: Shorter Songs for Worship from the Iona Community* (Glasgow: Wild Goose Publications, 1994).